THE CORAL REEF

A Colorful Web of Life

Philip Johansson

Enslow Elementary

an imprint of

Enslow Publishers, Inc.

40 Industrial Road
Box 398
Berkeley Heights, NJ 07922
USA

http://www.enslow.com

Library of Congress Cataloging-in-Publication Data

Johansson, Philip.
  The coral reef : a colorful web of life / Philip Johansson.
     p. cm. — (Wonderful water biomes)
  Includes bibliographical references and index.
  ISBN-13: 978-0-7660-2813-5
  ISBN-10: 0-7660-2813-5
  1. Coral reef ecology—Juvenile literature. I. Title.
  QH541.5.C7J64 2007
  577.7'89—dc22
                                                    2006017903

Printed in the United States of America

10 9 8 7 6 5 4 3 2 1

To Our Readers: We have done our best to make sure all Internet Addresses in this book were active and appropriate when we went to press. However, the author and the publisher have no control over and assume no liability for the material available on those Internet sites or on other Web sites they may link to. Any comments or suggestions can be sent by e-mail to comments@enslow.com or to the address on the back cover.

Every effort has been made to locate all copyright holders of material used in this book. If any errors or omissions have occurred, corrections will be made in future editions of this book.

Illustration Credits: Copyright © 1987, 1998 by Dover Publications, Inc.

Photo Credits: © 2006 Jupiterimages Corporation, p. 26 (sea slug), 44; ©1999, Artville, LLC, p. 13; Alexis Rosenfield//Photo Researchers, Inc., p. 42; Andrew Clarke/Photo Researchers, Inc., p. 17; Andrew J. Martinez/Photo Researchers, Inc., pp. 26 (sea cucumber), 29; Brandon Cole/Visuals Unlimited, p. 16; David Hall/Photo Researchers, Inc., pp. 26 (parrotfish), 38; David Wrobel/Visuals Unlimited, p. 26 (coral); Dr. D.P. Wilson/Photo Researchers, Inc., p. 24; Dr. Marli Miller/Visuals Unlimited, p. 15; Franklin Viola/ Animals Animals, p. 33; Fred McConnaughey/Photo Researchers, Inc., pp. 35, 43; Georgette Douwma/Photo Researchers, Inc., p. 40; Georgette Douwma/Photo Researchers, Inc., pp. 2, 9; James Crabbe, p. 7; Ken Lucas/ Visuals Unlimited, p. 37; Kjell B. Sandved/Visuals Unlimited, p. 34; Mary Beth Angelo/Photo Researchers, Inc., p. 14; Michele Westmorland/Animals Animals, p. 22; Reinhard Dirscherl/Visuals Unlimited, pp. 4, 30; Shutterstock, pp. 25, 26 (anemone); Steven Norvich/Visuals Unlimited, p. 18.

Front Cover: (clockwise from upper left) © 2006 Jupiterimages Corporation; Charles V. Angelo/Photo Researchers, Inc.; © Masa Ushioda/Visuals Unlimited; Mary Beth Angelo/Photo Researchers, Inc.

Back Cover: Reinhard Dirscherl/Visuals Unlimited

Dr. James Crabbe is a biochemist at the University of Bedfordshire, England, who studies the growth of coral colonies in Discovery Bay, Jamaica, and other sites around the world. The volunteers in Chapter 1 are from Earthwatch Institute, a nonprofit organization. Earthwatch supports field science and conservation through the participation of the public. See **www.earthwatch.org** for more information.

Table of CONTENTS

CHAPTER 1

Creature Castles 5

CHAPTER 2

The Coral Reef Biome 12

CHAPTER 3

Biome Communities 21

CHAPTER 4

Coral Reef Plants 27

CHAPTER 5

Coral Reef Animals 32

Words to Know 45

Learn More 47
(Books and Internet Addresses)

Index 48

THE CORAL REEF

Colorful coral reefs are full of life. This reef is in the Indian Ocean.

CREATURE CASTLES

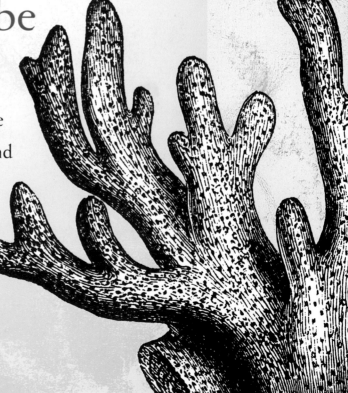

Dr. James Crabbe

and two volunteer assistants are
floating through clear, blue-green
water off the coast of Jamaica. The
only sound they hear is the hiss and
bubble of their scuba gear as they
pass over a fantastic landscape.
Mounds of bright coral of
every shape and size, separated

by patches of pure white sand, reach toward the divers. All around the coral, colorful fish dart in and out like clouds of confetti in the wind.

Coral reefs are bursting with life, more than any other part of the ocean. These reefs are massive mounds and ridges of stone under the sea. They are built by millions of tiny coral animals. Corals live together in groups called colonies, and it is these coral colonies that Dr. Crabbe and his field assistants are here to see.

When the divers reach a spot already marked with a bright pink ribbon, they float to a graceful stop. It is time to start their work. Signaling to each other with their hands, they mark out a one-meter square. The square goes around several coral colonies, each the size of a bowling ball. The divers begin to photograph the corals in the square. They measure each mound with a tape measure, and write numbers down on a waterproof writing board.

Coral Anniversary

"These coral colonies are only twenty years old or so," says Dr. Crabbe. The team has climbed out of the water into a small boat and pulled off their dripping equipment. The bright sun is reflecting off the blue water. Together, the team members study the measurements on the slate.

Dr. Crabbe's team members measure corals on the reef near Discovery Bay, Jamaica.

THE CORAL REEF

"They are much smaller than the ones we saw this morning, which were twice as old," Dr. Crabbe continues. Using the measurements they collected, he can get an idea of when each colony started to grow. The team can also learn about environmental causes, such as storms, that stop or slow the colonies' growth. "Last year we measured more than 1,200 coral colonies. Only one was from 1980, the same year a large hurricane hit Jamaica," he said. Hurricanes are one natural event that makes it very hard for new coral colonies to start growing.

Coral reefs also face new environmental impacts like climate change, increasing tropical storms, and pollution. Dr. Crabbe and his assistants want to know how these things affect the growth of coral colonies.

Sea of Plenty

Coral colonies are the backbone of coral reefs. The reefs, in turn, are home to thousands of species of plants and animals. Coral reefs around the

Golden damselfish are just one of many animals that live near coral reefs. This coral reef is in Thailand.

world contain more than 25 percent of all the kinds of plants and animals found in the ocean. Over 4,000 species of fish live among coral reefs. Thousands of kinds of plants and other animals, from tiny algae to bright worms and sea turtles, thrive in the coral reef biome.

Scientists like Dr. Crabbe study the colorful variety of life found on coral reefs. They explore the connections between coral reef plants and animals and their environment. This way, scientists can understand how these amazing coral kingdoms work, and how best to conserve them.

What Is a Biome?

Coral reefs are one kind of biome. A biome is a large region of Earth where certain plants and animals live. They survive in that biome because they are well suited to the environment found in that area.

Each biome has plants that may not be found in other biomes. Tall trees grow in forests, but not in deserts. In the ocean, marsh grass grows along the coast, but not in the middle of the ocean. The animals that eat these particular plants help form the living communities of a biome. Learning about a certain biome is a good way to explore how these communities work. In this book you will learn about the coral reef biome and the plants and animals that live there.

Chapter 2

The CORAL REEF BIOME

The amazing variety of plants and animals found on coral reefs is often compared to the rich life of rain forests. Like tropical rain forests, coral reefs are also found mostly in the tropics. The tropics are the warm seas just north and south of the equator. The corals that make up coral reefs need water temperatures from 70 to 85 degrees Fahrenheit

(21 to 29 degrees Celsius) to grow. They also live in places where ocean currents bring warm water to coastal areas, like Florida or southern Japan.

Coral reefs can be found along the coasts of more than 100 countries. All together, the world's coral reefs cover 110,000 square miles (285,000 square kilometers). That is about the size of the state of Nevada. Coral reefs

can only be found in shallow, coastal water less than 300 feet (100 meters) deep. The coral animals that build the reefs need sunlight to survive. The deeper the water, the more the sunlight is blocked. Even deeper than 60 feet (18 meters), most corals grow very slowly.

Most coral reefs grow in warm waters near the equator.

Tiny Builders

Coral reefs are made of a hard substance called limestone. The limestone comes from

The actual animals that make up the coral are tiny coral polyps. Here you see many individual star coral polyps. Each polyp lives inside its own skeleton, usually made of limestone.

corals—tiny, spineless animals related to jellyfish and anemones (uh NEH moh neez). Each tiny animal is called a polyp. A polyp is usually no thicker than a pencil and is shaped like a cup. A colony is made up of thousands of polyps, which produce layers of limestone homes for their protection. The colonies of different kinds of coral are built in different shapes. The colonies may be named for their shape, such as brain coral, elkhorn coral, staghorn coral, or mushroom coral.

Each coral reef is the product of thousands of colonies building onto the same area for thousands of years. Most coral reefs are between 5,000 and 10,000 years old, but some may be as old as 245 million years.

In addition to corals, other animals, such as clams, snails, and tube worms, add their hard shells to the reef. Even as the coral reefs build up, waves

This fringing reef is near the shore of **Grand Cayman.**

and storms tear them down. New colonies build upon the broken pieces. Tiny grains of broken reefs make up the pure white sand on tropical beaches.

There are many different types of coral reefs. Fringing reefs grow in shallow waters along the coast. Barrier reefs are separated from land by a stretch of open water, called a lagoon. Australia's Great Barrier Reef, the largest reef in the world, is 1,240 miles (2,000 kilometers) long. That's almost as long as the West Coast of the United States. Atolls are a third kind of reef. They form around

This atoll in the Caribbean Sea was once a volcanic island.

The Great Barrier Reef of Australia is home to more than 400 kinds of corals, 1,500 kinds of fish, and 4,000 types of clams, snails, and other mollusks.

volcanic islands. When an island sinks into the ocean, it leaves only a ring of coral around a blue lagoon.

Rich With Life

One of the reasons there are so many kinds of life on coral reefs is the variety of different

habitats, or places to live. Waves, ocean currents, and the animals themselves shape coral reefs into amazing forms with many levels. Holes and crevices provide shelter—and hiding places for hunters. These animals become meals for even larger animals. The colonies of tiny polyps provide food for many other animals.

Coral reefs are so full of life, they look like bustling cities. Fantastic animals of every color dart in and out of buildings of coral. Schools of fish cruise along the main streets. Parks of algae wave in the current. And over it all, the glittering sun shines through clear, tropical waters.

CORAL REEF FACTS

✓ **Tropical warmth:** Coral reefs grow in warm coastal waters, mostly in the tropics, where water temperature is always greater than 70 degrees Fahrenheit (20 degrees Celsius).

✓ **Land's edge:** Coral reefs need sunlight, so they are not found in water deeper than 300 feet (100 meters), such as the middle of the ocean.

✓ **Colonial living:** Coral reefs are built by coral polyps, which live in large colonies and produce limestone.

✓ **Reef shapes:** There are three basic kinds of reefs: fringing reefs, barrier reefs, and atolls.

✓ **Many homes:** Coral reefs provide a variety of habitats for other living things.

BIOME COMMUNITIES

Like biomes on land, coral reefs are made up of communities of plants and animals. Communities are groups of living things found together in the same place. Most living things have a role in the community. Some plants and animals depend on others, while others are living there just because they thrive in the same environmental conditions.

Energy Flow on the Coral Reef

Coral reef plants and algae trap the sun's energy. They use the energy to make sugars from water and carbon dioxide (a gas dissolved in the water). They store the sugars and use the energy to live and grow.

The sun shines over this reef in the National Marine Sanctuary in Key Largo, Florida. The plants in the reef get their energy from the sun.

Some animals, such as damselfish, rabbitfish, and sea urchins, eat algae or other ocean plants. Animals that eat only plants are called herbivores. Herbivores get their energy from plants. Animals that eat other animals are called carnivores.

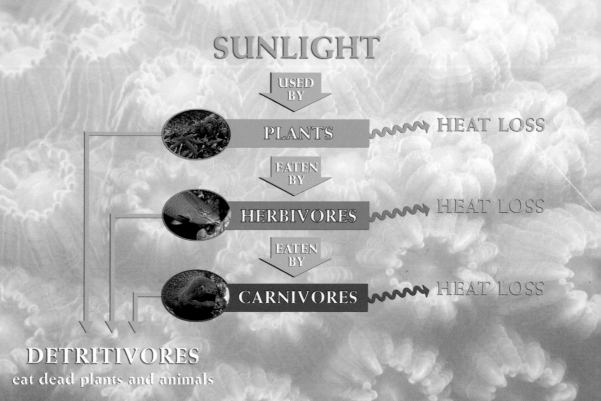

SUNLIGHT

USED BY

PLANTS — HEAT LOSS

EATEN BY

HERBIVORES — HEAT LOSS

EATEN BY

CARNIVORES — HEAT LOSS

DETRITIVORES
eat dead plants and animals

Barracudas, groupers, and other large reef fish are carnivores. Carnivores get their energy from eating the meat of other animals. Some animals, such as pufferfish, eat both plants and animals. They are called omnivores.

On the coral reef, another source of food is plankton. Plankton are tiny plants and animals that float through the water. Plankton animals eat plankton plants to get their nutrition. Larger coral

reef animals sift plankton plants and animals from the water for their food. These include corals, sea anemones,

sponges, and clams. These animals may then be eaten by even larger animals.

Some animals get their nutrition from plants and animals after they die. They are called detritivores (deh TRY tih vorz). They break down the dead plants and animals and capture nutrients, which are recycled through the coral reef system. Sea cucumbers, crabs, small crustaceans (kruh STAY shunz), and other bottom feeders do this job.

The Food Web

The flow of energy through the coral reef from the sun to plants to herbivores to carnivores to detritivores follows a pattern called a food web.

The food web connects the plants and animals of a community. It can be drawn to show who eats whom. For instance, damselfish eat algae. Groupers, in turn, eat damselfish. When a grouper dies, its body falls to the ocean floor, where detritivores such as crabs and worms can eat it. As the food web shows, most animals rely on several sources of food.

Together, plants and animals pass energy through the coral community. They also use some of the energy to live. At each stage of the food web, some energy is lost as the animals use it. It is lost in the form of heat. More energy from the sun needs to be trapped by plants to keep the coral reef communities alive.

Damselfish swim among a staghorn coral. Damselfish eat algae in the coral reef food web.

SOME PLANTS AND ANIMALS IN THE
CORAL REEF FOOD WEB

PLANTS	HERBIVORES	CARNIVORES

Eaten by → Eaten by →

Plankton plants

Plankton animals

Tube worms

Corals

Sea grass

Parrotfish

Triggerfish

Sea anemones

Sea urchins

Snails

Groupers

Green algae

Surgeonfish

Damselfish

Sea slugs

Red algae

Barracudas

Brown algae

Moray eels

DETRITIVORES

Sea cucumbers   **Crabs**

Chapter 4

CORAL REEF PLANTS

Most of the plants on coral reefs
are not easy to see. There are no sturdy trees
arching overhead or waving fields of flowers.
Large plants cannot grow on a coral reef.
Strong waves and storms are constantly
pounding the reef, making it a hard place
for most plants to grow. Also, there
is no rich soil to provide nutrients
for plant life. Reef plants do not have

◆ 27 ◆

large systems of roots and branches. They get their nutrients directly from the water.

Most plants on coral reefs are small. You have to look closely to find them among the showy corals. Some plants are so tiny that you cannot see them without a microscope. Some of these are the plankton plants, called phytoplankton (FYE toh plank tun). Tiny algae may be the most important part of the coral reef food chain. They live within the coral polyps themselves.

Living Together

Reef-building corals are actually part animal, part plant. The tiny polyps that live in coral colonies have even tinier algae living inside of them. Each polyp has thousands of the one-celled algae living in its body. The coral polyps and these one-celled plants need each other. The algae release food and oxygen for the polyps. The polyps release other nutrients that the algae use. This amazing relationship is called a

symbiosis (sim bye OH sis), which means "living together."

Similar one-celled algae are found in other coral reef animals. Some giant clams and sea slugs are home to these microscopic algae. These algae can be very colorful. Besides providing food for the giant clam, they also make bright patterns on its body.

Waving Leaves and Pink Cement

Larger algae can also be found living on coral reefs. Green, red, or brown algae have a simple, leafy shape. Unlike land plants, they don't need stiff stems to hold their leaves up. Their leaves float. They get their nutrients from the water around them. They often cover areas of the reef surface like a carpet.

Some algae are stony and stiff because they make limestone structures just like corals. Another unusual

The green color of these star corals is from algae. The algae live together with the coral polyps.

A blue sea star walks along sea grass in this coral reef in Indonesia.

plant is coralline alga. It looks more like pink cement than a plant, and it serves just that purpose. When parts of the reef crumble, coralline algae glue the rubble together. This makes a sturdy base for new coral colonies to settle upon.

Sea grass is a plant that has adapted to sea life. Sea grasses grow in the sandy patches between corals or in lagoons. Sea grass beds form low gardens of green. They make a good place for small animals to hide.

CORAL REEF PLANTS

✓ **Size is important:** Most coral reef plants are small and simple.

✓ **Invisible food:** Tiny plants called phytoplankton are carried over the reef by currents, providing food for many animals in the food web.

✓ **Live-in plants:** One-celled algae live inside the bodies of coral polyps, providing energy and nutrients for the corals.

✓ **Plant waves:** Carpets of green, red, and brown cover areas of the reef where corals have died or crumbled.

✓ **Coral look-alikes:** Some algae don't look like plants at all, but more like corals with crusty or stony surfaces.

CORAL REEF ANIMALS

Any reef can have thousands of different kinds of animals living on it, but finding them is not always easy. Many of the animals are small, like tiny worms, sea slugs, and shrimps. Others are well-hidden, like the clams burrowing in the sand or soldierfish hiding in crevices in the reef. Still others are hard to even recognize as animals. Soft corals and tube worms

look more like plants waving in the current. Sea anemones are animals that look like giant flowers.

Tiny Feast

Corals are the most common plankton eaters on the reef. Each coral polyp is a cup-shaped animal. Its mouth is surrounded by stinging tentacles, which help it to catch plankton. Many other plankton-eaters are similar to corals. Sea anemones

A school of soldierfish hides under an overhang in this coral reef.

◇ **33** ◇

A *Christmas tree tube worm off the coast of Puerto Rico looks more like a plant than an animal.*

are shaped like giant coral polyps, often in bright colors. They also catch plankton with their stinging tentacles and bring them to their mouth.

Sea horses use their tail to keep them in one place in the water. They sway in the current, sucking in plankton as it drifts by. Sponges are cup-shaped animals with pores, or holes, that they use to strain tiny bacteria out of the seawater. Sponges range from tiny to big enough to hold a human inside. Tube worms are worms that build protective tubes in which to live. They stick out their feathery legs to catch plankton. Clams, scallops, and other mollusks burrow in the sand. They pump water down through their bodies to sift out plankton.

With such a feast of plankton to be had, it is not

Bright chromis fish sit together over a coral colony. They eat plankton as it drifts by.

surprising that some fish eat this food too. Bright little fish called chromis hover together over coral colonies to hunt for plankton. Many other fish, such as wrasses, sergeant majors, and basslets, cruise over the reef in search of plankton during the day. Squirrelfish, soldierfish, and cardinalfish come out at night to get their share.

Algae Eaters

Another group of animals focuses its attention on the algae that grow on the reef surface. These plant eaters range from tiny, spiny sea urchins to great big parrotfish. All of them help keep algae from covering the reef. If too much algae covers the reef, it blocks the sunlight that coral colonies need to survive.

Plant-eating sea urchins are round and prickly like a pincushion. They crawl slowly across the reef on hundreds of tiny "tube" feet. A sea urchin grazes on algae just like a cow grazes on grass. Its mouth is

an opening on its underside, at the very center.
A variety of snails also eat algae. Most of these are
small, but some snails, like the queen conch,
are large.

Several kinds of fish also eat the reef's plentiful
algae. Surgeonfish travel in large schools, darting
down together to enjoy rich grazing spots. They are
called surgeonfish because they have tiny knifelike
barbs hidden at the base of their tail. The barbs
protect them from predators. Parrotfish are large,

*This flower
sea urchin is
beautiful, but
very venomous.
Sea urchins eat
algae on the
reef surface.*

brightly colored fish with beak-like mouths. They scrape the reef so hard with their tough teeth that you can actually hear them eating.

One surprising group of grazers is damselfish. These tough little fish actually guard their own private patch of algae from algae eaters. They will fearlessly defend their area against eager groups

Parrotfish use their beak-like mouths to scrape algae off the coral.

of surgeonfish or parrotfish, which are often ten times their size.

The Hunters

Many animals eat other animals on the coral reef. Some, such as carnivorous snails and worms, eat coral polyps. Butterfly fish and angelfish are the showiest coral eaters. These brightly colored fish have broad sides decorated with spots and stripes. They have little pointed mouths, perfect for nipping the tentacles off corals.

Some fish hunt for other small animals that live on the surface of the reef. They find shrimps, sea urchins, worms, brittle stars, and other prey. Triggerfish have the special ability to blow blasts of water that can turn a sea urchin over, exposing its spineless underside. Wrasses are cigar-shaped fish that feed on small animals. Blennies and gobies are tiny fish that eat still tinier animals from the reef's surface. They also eat algae and plankton.

Collared butterfly fish eat other animals on the coral reef, such as shrimp and coral polyps.

Certain wrasses and blennies find their tiny prey in a very special place: on the surface of other fish. These "cleaner fish" bravely pick off small animals attached to larger fish. The larger fish, sometimes dangerous predators like moray eels or groupers, calmly wait for the cleaners to do their work. There are also "cleaner shrimp" that serve the same role on some coral reefs.

At the top of the food web are the large predators that eat other fish. Some, like sharks, swim swiftly over the reef to pursue their prey. Sleek, shiny fish called jacks hunt in groups. Others, like barracudas or trumpetfish, surprise their prey. They hover silently over the reef, and then gobble up passing fish with a burst of speed. Some hunters wait on the bottom to attack their prey. Stonefish, scorpionfish, and toadfish often blend in with the reef. Moray eels are long and dangerous, with fanglike teeth. They hunt at night, hiding in holes in the reef and lunging out at fish as they pass.

Blacktip reef sharks are some of the hunters on the coral reef. These sharks are swimming near a reef in the Pacific Ocean near French Polynesia.

Coral Kingdom

Coral reefs provide important shelter and food for so many animals. Nearly one-fifth of all the kinds of fishes in the world live on coral reefs. However, these are only the most obvious residents. Many of the animals appear unusual to those of us living on land, from flower-like sea anemones to worms that look like feather dusters.

Scientists like Dr. James Crabbe are trying to understand how this fantastic habitat supports such plentiful life. While Dr. Crabbe studies how coral colonies grow, other scientists look at the partnership between coral polyps and their live-in one-celled algae. Still others explore who eats whom on the reef, or other animal interactions. With a better understanding of how coral reefs work, scientists will be able to suggest how to protect them from human impacts, such as pollution and global warming.

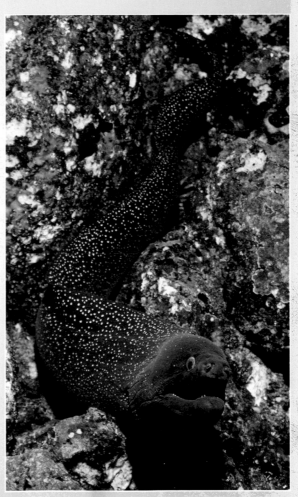

The moray eel is another predator in the coral reef food web. This eel slithers over rocks at a reef in the Galapagos Islands.

CORAL REEF ANIMALS

blenny

✓ **Odd shapes:** Coral reef animals are sometimes hard to recognize as animals. Soft corals, tube worms, and sea anemones are animals that look like plants.

✓ **Hovering food:** Many tiny animals simply wash over the reef. These plankton animals help feed the thousands of other reef animals.

✓ **Plant munchers:** Reef herbivores range from spiny sea urchins to great big parrotfish, which grind down the reef with their beaklike mouths.

✓ **Algae farmers:** Damselfish protect their own private patch of algae and defend it fiercely against other herbivores.

✓ **Coral snacks:** Some fish, such as butterfly fish and angelfish, nip the exposed tentacles off unsuspecting coral polyps.

✓ **Clean sweep:** Certain wrasses, blennies, and shrimps fill the role of cleaner. They pick harmful little animals off the bodies of larger fish.

✓ **Fish food:** The largest fish on the reef eat other fish, either by pursuing their prey or surprising them with a burst of speed.

atoll—A reef that once surrounded a volcanic island that has sunk, leaving a ring of coral.

barrier reef—A reef separated from land by a stretch of open water, called a lagoon.

biome—An area defined by the kinds of plants and animals that live there.

carnivore—An animal that eats other animals.

colony—A group of animals living together.

community—All the plants and animals living and interacting in any area.

coral—A tiny spineless animal, related to jellyfish and anemones, that lives in colonies and together build coral reefs.

coral reef—An undersea rock formation built by coral colonies that lay down layers of limestone.

detritivore—An animal that eats plants and animals after they have died.

food web—The web of life that allows the transfer of energy from the sun to plants to herbivores, carnivores, and finally to decomposers.

fringing reef—A reef that lines a coastal area.

habitat—The area where a certain plant or animal normally eats and finds shelter.

herbivore—An animal that eats plants.

mollusk—An animal with a soft body and a hard shell, such as clams, scallops, snails, octopuses, and squids.

nutrients—Chemicals that plants and animals need to live and grow.

omnivore—An animal that eats both plants and animals.

plankton—Tiny plants (phytoplankton) and animals that drift in the water.

polyp—An individual coral animal, shaped like a cup with tentacles.

reef—A large, rocky formation offshore that protects coastal areas and provides habitat for shallow-water plants and animals.

scuba—Equipment used by divers to breathe underwater.

tropics—The region of the earth close to the equator.

LEARN MORE

BOOKS

Bingham, Caroline. *Coral Reef.* New York: DK Publishing, 2005.

Gray, Susan H. *Coral Reefs.* Minneapolis: Compass Point Books, 2001.

Hirschmann, Kris. *Coral.* San Diego, Calif.: KidHaven Press, 2005.

Tocci, Salvatore. *Coral Reefs: Life Below the Sea.* New York: Franklin Watts, 2004.

INTERNET ADDRESSES

MacGillivray Freeman's Coral Reef Adventure.
    About Corals and Coral Reefs.
    http://www.coralfilm.com/about.html

Texas A&M University. *Ocean World. Coral Reefs.*
    http://oceanworld.tamu.edu/students/coral/

INDEX

A

algae, 10, 19, 22, 25, 28–29, 30, 36–39, 43
angelfish, 39
atolls, 16

B

barracudas, 23, 41
barrier reefs, 16
biomes, 10–11, 21
blennies, 39, 41
butterfly fish, 39, 44

C

carnivores, 22–24
chromis, 36
clams, 15, 24, 29, 32, 34
cleaner fish, 41
climate change, 8
communities, 11, 21, 25
coral colonies, 6–8, 14–16, 19, 20, 28, 30, 36, 43
coral polyps, 14, 19, 20, 28, 33–34, 39, 43, 44
coralline algae, 30
crabs, 24–25
crustaceans, 24

D

damselfish, 22, 25, 38, 44
detritivores, 24, 25

F

food web, 24–25, 41
fringing reefs, 16, 20

G

gobies, 39
Great Barrier Reef, 16
groupers, 23, 25, 41

H

habitats, 19, 20, 43
herbivores, 22, 24, 44
hurricanes, 8

L

limestone, 13, 14, 20, 29

M

moray eels, 41

N

nutrients, 24, 27–28, 29, 31

O

omnivores, 23

P

parrotfish, 36, 37, 39, 44
phytoplankton, 28, 31
plankton, 23–24, 28, 33–34, 36, 39, 44
pollution, 8, 43
predators, 37, 41
pufferfish, 23

R

rabbitfish, 22
rain forests, 12

S

sea anemones, 24, 33, 42, 44
sea cucumbers, 24
sea grass, 30
sea horses, 34
sea slugs, 29, 32
sea turtles, 10
sea urchins, 22, 36, 39, 44
sharks, 41
shrimps, 32, 39, 41, 44
snails, 15, 37, 39
soft corals, 32, 44
soldierfish, 32, 36
sponges, 24, 34
sunlight, 13, 20, 22, 25, 36
surgeonfish, 37, 39
symbiosis, 28–29

T

temperature, 12–13, 20
triggerfish, 39
tropics, 12, 20
tube worms, 15, 32, 34, 44

W

worms, 10, 25, 32, 39, 42
wrasses, 36, 39, 41, 44

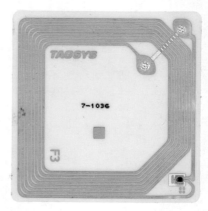